REMAIN IN LIGHT

REMAIN IN LIGHT

VISIONS OF HOMELAND AND DIASPORA

Gassia Armenian
EDITOR

FOWLER MUSEUM AT UCLA

LIBRARY OF CONGRESS CATALOGING-IN-PUBLICATION DATA
Names: Armenian, Gassia editor
Title: Remain in light : visions of homeland and diaspora / Gassia Armenian, editor.
Description: Los Angeles : Folwer Museum at UCLA, [2025] | Summary: "This book complements an exhibition of photographs at the Fowler Museum at UCLA (June 11–October 15, 2023) that endeavored to visualize the contemporary Armenian experience in the homeland and in Los Angeles-home to the largest Armenian population in diaspora. The first wave of immigrants came to California in the late 1800s; the second was spurred by the Armenian genocide of 1915; further Armenian migrants-from Soviet Armenia, the Middle East, Iran, and other countries-continue to find solace, pride, and connection in the traditions, customs, religion, language, and memories they brought with them. Sossi Madzounian, Ara Mgrdichian, and Ara Oshagan-three diaspora-born Armenian artists living in Los Angeles-shared their perspectives on the life of their people in the old world and the new, illuminating the evolving social fabric of Armenian life: survival in the homeland, the immigrant experience in diaspora, the rebirth of Armenian Americans on new soil. This book pairs their photographs with poems by Los Angeles-based poets Tina Demirdjian, Arminé Iknadossian, Arthur Kayzakian, Shahé Mankerian, and Raffi Joe Wartanian. The volume is a tribute to all these artists, and to Armenians across the globe"— Provided by publisher.
Identifiers: LCCN 2025013759 | ISBN 9780998044545 paperback
Subjects: LCSH: Armenians—Pictorial works—Exhibitions | Photography, Artistic—Exhibitions | Armenians--Poetry | LCGFT: Catalogs | Exhibition catalogs
Classification: LCC TR645.L72 F69 2025 | DDC 305.891/9920222--dc23/eng/20250506
LC record available at https://lccn.loc.gov/2025013759

Remain in Light: Visions of Homeland and Diaspora (June 11–October 15, 2023) was organized by the Fowler Museum at UCLA and curated by Gassia Armenian.

This publication was supported by a generous gift from The Esrailian Family.

LENDERS TO THE EXHIBITION:
Armenian Archaeology Department of the UCLA Cotsen Institute of Archaeology

FRONT COVER:
SOSSI MADZOUNIAN
(b. 1957, Beirut, Lebanon)
The Light Under Dark Clouds (detail),
October 2015

PREVIOUS SPREAD:
SOSSI MADZOUNIAN
Prayers (detail)
October 2015

RIGHT:
ARA MGRDICHIAN
Anahid Redux (detail), 2019

Contents

Foreword

SILVIA FORNI

How to visualize and evoke the longing and belonging texturing Armenian history and experience? How to narrate the sense of rootedness and resilience shaping communities forced out of their homeland? How to depict the uniqueness of a mostly transnational yet deeply connected community?

The history of Armenian people is one of turmoil, violence, and forced migration. It is also the story of remarkable resilience and strength, rooted in a sense of home that transcends location, and ability to thrive and blossom throughout multiple displacements and diasporas. Told from the vantage point of three photographers and five poets currently living in Los Angeles, the story unfolding on the following pages demonstrates the complex layering of personal and communal identity, of rootedness and alienation intersecting in persistent yet not always predictable ways. Through images and words, *Remain in Light: Visions of Homeland and Diaspora* evokes darkness and light, pain and hope, destruction and renewal. The language does not construct a linear narrative but conjures up the need to remember and hold on to a sense of belonging while letting go of the pain; to remain anchored while continuing to move forward; to stay connected to one's community while changing and evolving.

Ultimately, *Remain in Light* pays tribute to people, places, and images that define the Armenian diasporic experience, which exists in the liminal space between the homeland and the new homes Armenians have built in the greater Los Angeles area. Yet despite its specificity, it is a story that resonates with immigrant people from all over the world, as all migrants live the tension between different ideas of home and belonging.

This exhibition, its accompanying programs, and the present book would have not been possible without the indefatigable commitment that Gassia Armenian, the Fowler Museum's Curator and Research Associate, has brought to the project. She not only curated the show and the public programs but also promoted the initiative across LA, making sure that people in the community felt included and welcome at the Fowler Museum. Our sincere gratitude also goes to Tina Demirdjian, Arminé Iknadossian, Arthur Kayzakian, Sossi Madzounian, Shahé Mankerian, Ara Mgrdichian, Ara Oshagan, Raffi Joe Wartanian for believing in this project; and to Amy McFarland for transforming their vision of homeland, immigration, and rebirth into the materiality of this book.

I would also like to thank the members of the Fowler staff for their contributions. Marina Belozerskaya managed this volume with keen editorial skills. Rachel Raynor and her team—Isabella Kelly-Ramirez, Jenny Hirons, Jeanette Saunders, and Amy Rubinstein—provided the technical support and installation expertise for the exhibition. Michal Broomfield, Don Cole, Kathy DiGenova, Amy Landau, Libby O'Kane, and Hannah Yoo supported in various ways the making of the exhibition, the public programs, and the production of this volume. Last but not least, we are grateful to Kristine Martirosyan-Olshansky, UCLA Cotsen Institute of Archaeology, Director of the Armenian Lab; Melissa Bilal, The Promise Chair in Armenian Music, Arts, and Culture and director of Armenian Music Program at the UCLA Herb Alpert School of Music, for partnering on programs and writing for this book; and to The Esrailian Family whose generous gift fully supported this publication.

SILVIA FORNI
Shirley and Ralph Shapiro Director
Fowler Museum at UCLA

Prelude

MELISSA BILAL

This term (Spring 2025) at UCLA, I am teaching an Ethnomusicology course titled "Music and Minorities in Turkey" to a brilliant group of undergraduates from diverse majors and backgrounds. This week, we discussed how songs accumulate layers of affective histories on their musical and poetic bodies and thus become resources for remembrance. Our focus was my community, the Bolsahays, Armenians of Istanbul, for whom "music is a connection to a place and past, a connection that is at times unshakable" to quote Cheryl A. Wall, it is "a metaphor for the unspeakable: what cannot be said both because it is too painful or dangerous to express in words and because no one could hear or understand the words if they could be found." I shared with my students my personal experience of growing up in Turkey, where my past was available to me in public only through its repeated denial, and in private, through the fragmented stories and silences I inherited from my genocide surviving family. As we studied the gendered role of music in Armenian everyday resistance against repressive minority and memory politics in Turkey, our class conversation continued to an exploration of "Tsitsernakaberd / Dzidzernagapert" (Fortress of the Swallow), the name of the Armenian Genocide memorial in Yerevan, and its relation to the popular song titled "Dzidzernagin Puyne" (Swallow's Nest). Based on a pre-genocide era poem, this children's song, which is also often sung as a lullaby, tells the story of a swallow singing and reminiscing of her old home while building the new one, which one day she finds ruined. Associated with the memory of the genocide today, this song also gives meaning to this site of commemoration by breaking the colonial binary of "tangible" vs. "intangible" and by inviting its visitors to add their own songs and stories to this "nest" of memory to practice collective remembrance in its multiplicity and plurality. Music gives us tools to craft creative and non-normative ways of relating to belonging and loss. Arts in general enable us to express complexities and address power dynamics. As I witnessed my students turn our classroom into a transformative space of exchanging their critical, sensitive, and self-reflexive thoughts on awareness, responsibility, and solidarity, I asked myself: isn't this the very connection between art and education that both empower us to transgress boundaries? Exactly for this reason, when we, UCLA Armenian Music Program, were invited to share our music during *Janyak* exhibition at the Fowler Museum, curated by Gassia Armenian and showcasing Marie Pilibossian's needle lace work testifying to her life experience as a genocide survivor and first-generation immigrant Armenian woman in the U.S., I knew that this collaboration was going to be the first of many. As I write this prelude inspired by voices and perspectives presented by the photography artists and poets featured in this volume, I would like to express my appreciation and wish to continue our collective efforts to bring visibility to the intersectional Armenian experience in Los Angeles and to build an inclusive community around Armenian music, literature, and art.

April 24, 2025

MELISSA BILAL
UCLA Herb Alpert School of Music
Assistant Professor of Ethnomusicology
Assistant Professor of Music
Promise Chair in Armenian Music, Arts, and Culture
Director of the Armenian Music Program

Introduction

GASSIA ARMENIAN

On November 11, 2022, I opened the cover of a blank book. I created a mental outline for a photography exhibition at the Fowler Museum at UCLA and began to transform the story in my mind into action.

A granddaughter of Armenian genocide survivors, I was born and grew up in Lebanon, a country "that was not ours." The dream of an independent homeland has been a constant in my life. As a diaspora Armenian, I learned about Armenia through books, maps, and stories of those who once lived there. It was a mythical reality until Armenia gained its independence from the Soviet Union on September 21, 1991.

Without Soviet restraints, Armenians of the diaspora could visit the homeland to experience the magnetic powers of the soil, the water, and the air. As immigrants, we returned home to feel viscerally the epic tales of victory, the horrors of oppression, and the healing power of freedom. Were we truly free? Were we no longer immigrants? Were we now free immigrants?

Immigration has meant constant movement in the lives of worldwide Armenians, always seeking new horizons of safety, opportunity, and light. Did they understand what awaited them ahead? Not really. Rebirth around the world, on new lands, tested the amount of light we could carry in our suitcases. The process of rebirth proved as difficult, if not more so, as the first time each of us left our mother's womb. It felt treacherous.

Yes. Roses beyond the horizon had thorns, too.

The exhibition I envisioned would have photographs conveying the contemporary Armenian experience in Armenia; in Artsakh—also known as Nagorno-Karabagh, an autonomous Armenian territory annexed to Azerbaijan in 1921 by Stalin; and in Los Angeles. On November 11, 2022, I chose to share my vision with three talented Armenian American photographers: Sossi Madzounian, Ara Mgrdichian, and Ara Oshagan. They served as my litmus test. They believed my vision could manifest, though it still felt like fiction or a dream, but they did not dismiss my idea. Within a week, all three visited the Fowler Museum to see and get a feel for the space where their work might hang if my hope came to fruition through their skills and talents. Subsequently, they submitted hundreds of photographs that reflected themes of homeland, immigration, and rebirth.

Madzounian, Mgrdichian, and Oshagan draw their inspiration from a combination of memories, life experiences, personal preferences, and individual philosophies. Each acknowledges the existence of two and sometimes three homelands. They grew up with the eternal yet impossible dream of witnessing an independent Armenia, free from Soviet bondage. When that hope became a reality in 1991, the three photographers did not hesitate to arm themselves with their cameras and travel from Los Angeles to Armenia and Artsakh to document the post-Soviet reality. They captured many variations on the theme of survival in the homeland and rebirth in Los Angeles County, which is now home to nearly half a million residents of Armenian descent. Their work also highlighted the forward momentum of the new generations empowered by their cultural identity and heritage.

On June 10, 2023, the exhibition *Remain in Light: Visions of Homeland and Diaspora*, featuring the work of Madzounian, Mgrdichian, and Oshagan, opened in the Goldenberg galleria at the Fowler Museum with 47 photographs offering a vivid essay on the contemporary Armenian experience in Armenia, Artsakh, and Los Angeles. The photographers created a luminous connection between the immigration process and the rebirth on foreign shores. The exhibition offered the viewers a chance to visualize that quest for light. Did it lead toward a better life or highlight fear and loss?

Los Angeles has the largest Armenian community outside of Armenia, with several high schools covering all grades, as well as many pre-kindergartens and kindergartens. More than 20 churches, 10 cultural and sports organizations, the Ararat-Eskijian Museum, and many professional associations, such as the Armenian Bar Association, the Armenian American Medical Society, the Armenian Engineers and Scientists Association, the Armenian Relief Society, and others cater to socio-cultural endeavors and needs of this population.

Armenians began to immigrate to Los Angeles in the late 1800s and early 1900s, following the Hamidian Massacres, a series of atrocities organized and carried out against the Armenians by the government of the Ottoman Sultan Abdul Hamid II. These attacks set the precedent and a blueprint for the Armenian genocide of 1915, perpetrated by the Ottoman government—the systematic destruction of the Armenian people living in the Ottoman Empire. The survivors were sheltered in the Middle East as a first destination and then in the United States and other countries. Political instability in the Middle East from the 1950s to the 1980s generated a third wave of immigrants fleeing from Egypt, Syria, Iraq, Lebanon, Iran, and Turkey to the U.S. The dissolution of the Soviet Union in 1991 contributed to the fourth influx of Armenians to Los Angeles. Thus, over the course of the 20th century, Armenians from countries troubled by political, religious, and human rights violations found refuge and the possibility of a new start in California.

What did these immigrants bring with them? What could they carry along? Traditions, customs, religion, language, memories, and, most of all, hope that they were moving toward a better life. They held fast to their faith that they would find and remain in light in Los Angeles.

The Goldenberg galleria at the Fowler Museum is a square corridor surrounding an atrium. Each wall has two large panels, often dedicated to photography exhibitions. *For Remain in Light*, the first panel was given to the photograph of Mount Ararat by Sossi Madzounian along with a case displaying 8,000-year-old soil from Masis Blur on the Ararat plain, lent by the Armenian Archaeology Department of the UCLA Cotsen Institute of Archaeology. The lab's director, Kristine Martirosyan-Olshansky, provided a scientific explanation and caption for the soil.

Fig. 1

SOSSI MADZOUNIAN
(b. 1957, Beirut, Lebanon)
The Light Under Dark Clouds
October 2015
Araratian Plateau, Vayotz Dzor Province, Armenia,
on the way to the Areni

(objects inside the case)

MASIS BLUR (Մասիս Բլուր; Masis mound), Armenia
"Heavy fraction" from an 8,000-year-old farming community, collected in 2018. Soil, small rocks, small obsidian tools, animal teeth and bones (sheep and goat). Loan of the UCLA Cotsen Institute of Archaeology, Armenian Lab, Research Program for Armenian Archaeology

These soil samples were field-collected in 2018 at the archaeological site of Masis Blur (Masis mound, Մասիս Բլուր) in the Ararat Valley, in the foothills of Mount Ararat. According to Kristine Martirosyan-Olshanksy, excavation director, this soil is the "heavy fraction" and did not require a special export permit. Archaeologists use the flotation process to retrieve burnt plant remains, small bones, and small tools from the soil, which reveals the subsistence practices and day-to-day activities of ancient communities. During this process, the soil is poured into a bucket of water. The burnt botanical remains float to the surface and are called "light fraction." The rocks, beads, small tools, and bones sink to the bottom and are called "heavy fraction." The U.S. Department of Agriculture must issue a special permit for the import of "light fraction," while "heavy fraction" can be imported without a permit.

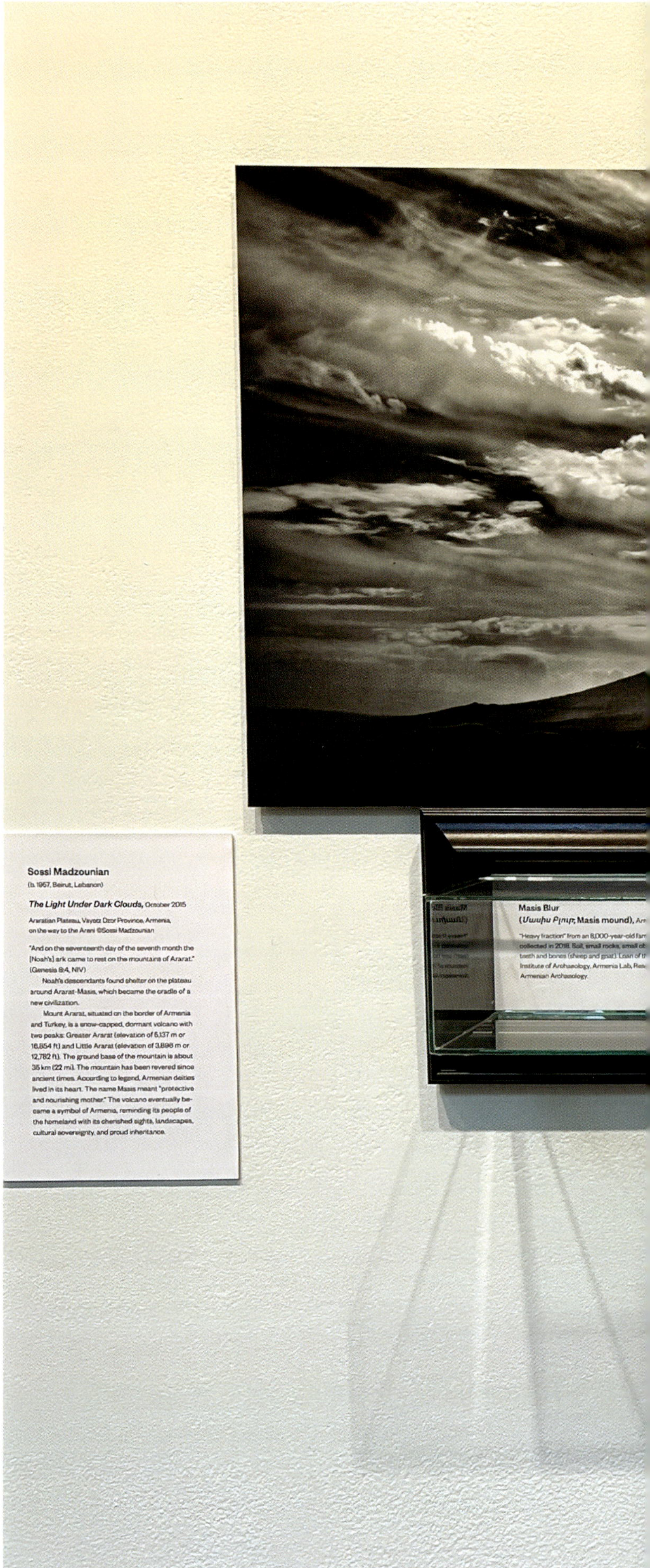

were field-collected in 2018 at the
of Masis Blur (Masis mound,
Valley, in the foothills of Mount Ararat.
Martirosyan-Olshanksy, excavation
the "heavy fraction" and did not require
Archaeologists use the flotation
burnt plant remains, small bones, and
soil, which reveals the subsistence
practices and day-to-day activities of ancient communities.
During this process, the soil is poured into a bucket of water.
The burnt botanical remains float to the surface and are
called "light fraction." The rocks, beads, small tools, and
bones sink to the bottom and are called "heavy fraction."
The U.S. Department of Agriculture must issue a special
permit for the import of "light fraction," while "heavy
fraction" can be imported without a permit.

Mount Ararat, situated on the border of Armenia and Turkey, is a snow-capped, dormant volcano with two peaks: Greater Ararat (elevation of 5,137 meters or 16,854 feet) and Little Ararat (elevation of 3,896 meters or 12,782 feet). The ground base of the mountain is about 35 km (22 mi). The mountain has been revered since ancient times. According to legend, Armenian deities lived in its heart. The name Masis meant "protective and nourishing mother." The volcano eventually became a symbol of Armenia, reminding its people of the homeland with its cherished sights, landscapes, cultural sovereignty, and proud inheritance. Kristine Martirosyan-Olshanksy, excavation director of the archaeological site of Masis Blur (Masis Mound, Մասիս Բլուր) in the Ararat Valley, in the foothills of Mount Ararat, has collected the soil samples included in the exhibition in 2018.

Ara Oshagan's photographs (pages 22-41) graced the second and third gallery panels. Oshagan describes himself as:

> an intersectional artist and curator working in photography, collage, archive, endangered language, film, book-arts, and installation art. Vectored by my own personal history, I am a documentarian as well as a conceptual artist. A descendant of communities who were deracinated from their indigenous lands by the Armenian genocide in 1915, I was born in Lebanon and displaced by civil war as a youth. I am diasporic and live in the wake of multi-generation displacement and dispossession.

I view him as a magician who has captured moments in the lives of Armenians that can be transcribed into chapters of past, present, and future histories.

The fourth and fifth panels held the photographs of Sossi Madzounian (pages 44-64). She was commissioned by the Smithsonian Institution's Center for Folklife and Cultural Heritage division to go to Armenia and photo-document the Areni wine caves dating back 6,000 years. For Madzounian,

> Being part of the Armenian diaspora in Los Angeles has brought forth conflicting emotions of complete belonging and utter loss—a feeling I have navigated throughout my dual identity existence.

A high priestess of equilibrium, able to create harmony between light, natural elements, and humans in her photos, Madzounian has reconfigured and captured spaces where Armenians can find solace and peace.

Photographs of Ara Mgrdichian (pp. 67-87) occupied the sixth and seventh panels. If you asked Mgrdichian about his identity, he would say,

> Armenia and Armenians have always been trans-territorial and transnational, yet thoroughly indigenous. We have always lived between disparate physical and metaphysical worlds, cultures, and societies—bridging and being bridged in the process.

For Ara, the wordsmith, the world started with the alphabet, then reconfigured into words, and finally into frozen images or photographs.

The eighth panel featured a photo album of my favorite images from the portfolios of Madzounian, Mgrdichian, and Oshagan (pp. 90-108), especially the ones that stood apart from the rest. Did they want to speak up louder than other photos? The image of the folk dancers (p. 105), for example, felt as if they were uniting all Armenians around the world—since all Armenians, from the age 5 to 95 and even more, cherish our traditional dances, continuing centuries-old customs.

The final image of the exhibition had a special symbolic value. It showed an exploded pomegranate, which stood for rebirth and regeneration of all Armenian communities around the world (p. 108).

The artists actively participated in the exhibition's creation. In addition to selecting their photographs, they shared their voices, contextualized their visions, and composed the captions for their images. However, I wanted to add a surround-sound depth and breadth to the photographs—through the velocity of the words made possible by poetry.

On June 29, 2023, I contacted Shahé Mankerian, an acclaimed poet who serves on the board of the International Armenian Literary Alliance. I shared with him my idea of creating a public event: "Poetry Under the Stars" that would bring together Armenian American poets. A vision that hovered in my mind was the traditional Lebanese Zajal poetry recitation—since the photographers and most of the poets were born in the Middle East—at which poets gather for a conversation through poems that they compose on the spot.

Mankerian arrived at the Fowler Museum with a powerful team of poets: Tina Demirdjian, Arminé Iknadossian, Arthur Kayzakian, and Raffi Joe Wartanian. Together, we viewed the photographs, talked, shed tears, laughed, and hugged. The poets liked the edgy and non-conformist images on display and the almost palpable feel of incense burning in front of an altar in one of the photographs. We shook hands on an event that would take place on September 27, 2023. On that day, the melody of poems and blessings from the churches in the photographs, imbued with oud music performed by Raffi Joe Wartanian, created a magical atmosphere. All, of course, was done under the auspices of the constellation Orion or Haik, patriarch of all Armenians for millennia. That special event planted the seeds for the present book. Why not combine the photographs and the poems of the eight Armenian American artists who amazingly enough have expressed the same sentiments of outrage at the injustices suffered by the Armenians and voiced the same demands for restitution? The micro-study created by one small group of diaspora-born Armenian photographers residing in Los Angeles gave an overall image of Armenian communities and inspired the poets.

But before the poetry event on September 27, 2023, came September 19, 2023. On that day, the Fowler hosted a special guest who had come for a private tour of the exhibitions *Janyak, Armenian Art of Knots and Loops* and *Remain in Light: Visions of Homeland and Diaspora* with the museum's director Silvia Forni. A few moments into the visit, our guest announced: "They attacked Artsakh last night"—referring to Azerbaijan. That calamity uprooted 120,000 Armenians from their homes in Artsakh in one day, forcing them to migrate to the Armenian mainland, leaving behind homes, orchards, farm animals, schools, churches, and ancestral graves.

Over the course of the exhibition, many personal links between the artworks and museum visitors emerged. One guest recognized in one of the photographs the woman who had given her the first job in the U.S. Another's niece had attended martial arts classes at Olymp Studio pictured in the exhibition. A third person noted that it was his father who had opened the first Armenian bookstore in Hollywood, featured in the show. For four months, visitors communed with the transcendental images from Armenia's past and present captured in the photographs of ancient monuments and contemporary scenes; and with the spirits of our ancestors floating among the clouds and swaying in the fields behind churches. The patina of visitors' memories and experiences enriched the exhibition. Now, each photograph comes to life further through an accompanying poem.

Organizing the pages of this book was almost an automatic process, as if the words and images were waiting to be paired. It took less than two hours to spread the printouts of the photographs on the floor of my living room, walk among them, and combine them with the poems that seemed to speak to them. The images and the poems merged as if coming from ancestral consciousness.

By October 15, 2023, the closing day of the exhibition, the history of Armenia and Artsakh changed, once again, as it had done so many times, and images of Artsakh in the exhibition no longer stood as patrimony of the Armenian nation and Armenian people. Within the span of the show, Artsakh—part of the Armenian homeland reflected in the photographs—was no longer officially identified as Armenian, having fallen under the oppressive rule of Azerbaijan, shocking the Armenian communities in Los Angeles and around the world. How could other nations remain silent in the face of ethnic cleansing, forced migration, and occupation of a sovereign territory?

As I arranged the poems in this book, the evening when they were read at the Fowler Museum was vivid in my mind, as were the voices of the poets, whose words grace this introduction and the following pages.

"While it is maddening for us," observed poet Arthur Kayzakian, "to compare death camps to poetry, there is resonance in their comparisons. So today, we will continue discussing the sound of a rifle and poetry by investigating how death travels." Thus Kayzakian, Los Angeles-based poet of Iranian Armenian heritage, set the stage for his poems, which carry electricity and energy as they take shape in his "Lecture Hall: Physics: Velocity/Speed of Sound and Poetry" (p. 23)" or in such verbal images as, "From fire bluster and windows rattled by gunfire..." ("Exiled: Los Angeles...," p. 75).

Tina Demirdjian walked to her bedroom closet, opened the door, and reached for the bundle carefully placed on the top shelf. She brought it down and untied it. Saved for a special day, memories of her grandmothers rushed out and poured onto a page:

> "Where are you from?"
> the old man asked,
> leaned over
> in his white cotton shirt
> to fix the bins
> in this tiny space.
> "Queens," I answered.
> The other small man
> with a gold tooth
> clicked his tongue
> in disapproval.
> "No! Where are you from?"
> "New York," I answered,
> again in Armenian.
> Their eyes narrowed
> And heads now at a slant.
> So, I replied:
> "Istanbul, Bolis."
> They waited, the minivan
> Now silent.
> * * *
> "Where is your family from?"
> "Gesaria, my family is from Gesaria."
> "Ah, now I know who you are,"
> they said simultaneously and smiled.
> It was my ancestors
> they were looking for." (page 55)

The sultry melodies of the oud had enveloped the poetry reading. My gaze tried to follow each note, each phrase, each refrain. Raffi Joe Wartanian—the Kousan—the troubadour, strung the words and the notes together to capture moments "Between Time and Space." Suddenly, "Disco Datev" made a youthful and innocent appearance on the horizon of destiny (p. 71). No! No one should forget that:

> Cookie Monster came for the sweets.
> He stayed for the genocide.
> Superman saw the slaughter
> in the name of the father, the son,
> the holy . . . (p. 80)

Regardless of the condition or location of exile, the immigrants reached the new homeland with a couple of suitcases filled with stories nostalgic for the past, with the whistling sounds of bullets crisscrossing right over the heads of saints, and, of course, their heads. If you ask Arminé Iknadossian, Arminé with the peridot heart, as she refers to herself, about how her mother coped with her new home in Pasadena, in a new country away from her roots left behind in Beirut, she would say:

> Mother stirs the soup.
> Says she smells the Mediterranean.
> A Monarch butterfly appears from behind
> a dish rack
> on her way to Mexico or San Simeon,
> glides from faucet to shoulder to ladle.
> Together, they listen to the bubbling of
> the ocean. (p. 76)

Arminé with the peridot heart would also warn:

> Blue glass eyes ward off evil,
> so hang one from your rearview mirror
> and pin it on a newborn baby.
> If they break, a tragedy has been avoided.
> (p. 63)

That is exactly what I said to my daughter a few years ago when she told me in a horrified voice that the blue bead that her grandma had given her and that had hung on her front door, shattered by itself without any human or outside interference. I said, "A tragedy has been avoided."

Adjacent to Los Angeles, Pasadena is home to a vibrant Armenian community. Who would say that a teenage boy growing up during the Civil War of Beirut, who saw death in the eye—many forms of death—would be looking straight into the eyes of life, of many burgeoning lives in Pasadena? Yet that is what Shahé Mankerian—poet, educator, humanist, and principal of Saint Gregory Armenian School in Pasadena—has been doing through his verses. He looks straight into the smiling eyes of a new generation of Armenian children born on the host land of Los Angeles County. Could he forget what he saw as a teenager? Could crossing the ocean cleanse his memories? Could he wish he were forgetful? Maybe. Forgetfulness has a memory of its own, and Shahé looks straight into its eyes and soul.

She might finally forget
my name when she's dicing
onions on a chopping block.
For now, Mother can't pinpoint
My daughter's birthday.
She forgets to swallow
her blood pressure pills,
so she leaves church early.
After she calms her heart, she drinks
Turkish coffee.
She can't sleep at night
Because, when she closes her eyes,
she remembers everything. (p. 98)

Regardless of where they live, Armenians gather spiritually at the foothills of Mount Ararat, recharge their inner light, and forge ahead through dark times. Ara Mgrdichian, Sossi Madzounian, Ara Oshagan, Shahé Mankerian, Arminé Iknadossian, Tina Demirdjian, Arthur Kayzakian, and Raffi Joe Wartanian have added their patinas to the photographs presented at the Fowler Museum. This book is a tribute to all these artists, and to Armenians at home and in diaspora.

In the final image of the exhibition, a pomegranate explodes, its arils claiming justice and casting the light of rebirth and regeneration on Armenians around the world (p. 109). Together, in unity, we turn the pages of this book and carry the light into the future. Լույսով մենք (looysov menak).

Photographs and Poems

Fig. 2
ARA OSHAGAN
Holy Liturgy
Gantzasar Monastery
(13th century), Vank Village,
Artsakh, 1999 ©Ara Oshagan

"My father accompanied me on this visit to Gantzasar Armenian monastery. We had traveled thousands of miles from our diasporic homes to Artsakh, and we traveled another hour and a half by taxi over muddy roads... We climbed the last incline by foot because the taxi got stuck in the mud. It was a kind of secular pilgrimage. Upon entering the monastery, I was immediately overtaken and paralyzed by the combination of the ancient monastery walls, the ephemeral light, and the deeply resonant voices of the choir. It was a deeply spiritual moment for me, an out-of-body experience. For a long time, I just stood unmoving, bathed in this ethereal and mystical moment. My father had a similar experience. After a while, I did manage to take a few pictures and this was one of them—near the end of the holy liturgy."

Lecture Hall: Physics: Velocity / Speed of Sound and Poetry

BY ARTHUR KAYZAKIAN

While it is maddening for us to compare death camps to poetry, there is resonance in their comparisons. So, today, we will continue discussing the sound of a rifle and poetry by investigating how death travels. We know the speed of a bullet will increase its mass, and its calculation depends on its projective velocity, which considers many variables: air friction against the bullet, atmospheric pressure of clouds, sun-beaten temperatures, and so on. Since a bullet travels 1200 miles per second, which means the muzzle velocity moves faster than the speed of sound, which means a bullet moves through time quicker than a bell or a horn or a lullaby, you are struck before you hear your mother's laughter leave the barrel.

TEFALL

Fig. 3
ARA OSHAGAN
Lachin, Artsakh, 2006

"In 2006, I traveled through the Lachin corridor of Artsakh—the only direct link of the region to Armenia. I visited towns and villages all the way down near the Iranian border, where the effects of war from the 1990s are still felt. In 2020, the state of Azerbaijan launched a full-scale military attack on the indigenous Armenian communities of Artsakh. With superior funding and training, they captured and colonized vast regions of Artsakh. In 2023, Azerbaijan placed the remaining Armenian population under a blockade by closing off the Lachin corridor—attempting to ethnically cleanse the region of all Armenians. The blockade continues today (as of March 2023)."

On September 19, 2023, the Azeri government continued its ethnic cleansing scheme of all Armenians from Artsakh, with the forced migration of 120,000 men, women, and children.

Fig. 4
ARA OSHAGAN
Wedding at Hotel Eclectica, Vank Village, Artsakh, 2006

"This hotel was built in the shape of a ship by a local entrepreneur and millionaire from Vank village. The locals call it 'Titanic' after the famed Hollywood movie. The hotel has an artificial waterfall and the only zoo in Artsakh. Its vivid yellow, tan, blue, and green stand in stark contrast to the surrounding lush vegetation and landscape."

Fig. 5
ARA OSHAGAN
April 24, 2002

April 24, the day of the Armenian genocide of 1915, commemorated by a march in East Hollywood, Little Armenia.

Why I Am Resourceful

BY ARMINÉ IKNADOSSIAN

Aintab, Turkey: 1915

Crouched behind a wagon,
my great grandmother, only 12,

can smell benzine, burning hair —
shouts of hungry men, lust in their curses.

Yeranouhi, which means wish,
smears charcoal on her pretty face

like a dutiful daughter, watches
as her mother hides her young brother,

rolling him gently into a small carpet.

Fig. 6
ARA OSHAGAN
Wedding Reception
Arbat Palace, Glendale, CA, 2004

A Day at an Armenian Wedding

BY TINA DEMIRDJIAN

Another wedding and I hardly
know the bride and groom.
My brother is seated to my left
but all the other faces
are unfamiliar.

Pink and white tables
scatter the ballroom
the band plays standard
wedding music
for couples to dance
cheek to cheek.
A short chubby man
with a balding head
dances with a pretty
16-year-old girl,
another couple
in their seventies
dance slower
than the beat of the music
everyone else
is loudly chatting.
Sitting to my right
is an old woman
wearing a burgundy dress
who doesn't speak English
so I introduce myself
in Armenian
and she smiles gently
and asks me again,

what is your name?

Tina Demirdjian I reply.
Her eyes hidden
in her face slightly widen.

Demirdjian she repeats
many times and asks,
where is your family from?
Istanbul I answer.
Her hands grip the pink napkin
next to mine.
And before they moved
to the city? her voice hesitates.
Gesaria,
my family is from Gesaria.
The old woman smiles again
but lowers her head and I see
her right hand clench
her plate and turn it,
slowly after a few seconds
she looks up at me again

what is your father's first name?

Hagop, I answer and turn
around for a moment to watch
the short balding man still dancing
with the 16-year-old bridesmaid.

Your father's name is Hagop
she repeats over and over.
I turn around and see the old
face of a little girl staring at me.

Yes, yes I say and watch her shake.
My brother's name was Hagop, too
and she takes my hand.

I was eight years old in the beginning
of the Armenian Genocide in 1915.
My parents were killed. All I had left
was my brother, Hagop.
Our name was Demirdjian, too.
We lived in the closest town
to Gesaria. My brother and I
were taken to someone's house.
When we got there they took Hagop
away. They said they'd bring him
back, but they never did.

Her tears now lay in the crevices
of her wrinkles
as she clutches my arm
and looks directly into my eyes:

I am 80 years old and I've
never given up hope.

Fig. 7
ARA OSHAGAN
Scouts
Los Angeles, CA, 2003

There are two major scout troops in the Western Region of the United States. The Armenian General Athletic Union and Scouts (Homenetmen), and the Armenian General Benevolent Union scouts. The Homenetmen alone has over 3,000 members.

In addition to peer bonding, outdoor activities, and survival skills, the scouts engage in community outreach to help ensure a better quality of life for all human beings.

Fig. 8
ARA OSHAGAN
Men Kissing
Burbank, CA, 2002

Thank God for Judas

BY SHAHÉ MANKERIAN

During the Passion play tryouts,
even Suzan, who loved to bite boys,
wanted to play Jesus. She insisted
her long hair and the contour

of her waist was perfect
for the cross. But she was fat,
and no one dared to say that
to her face. Even Mrs. Shnorig

had difficulty dissuading her.
Suzan's parents were lawyers
and controlled the principal
with letters of threat. I didn't care.

I secretly liked Suzan; she smelled
like buttery croissants when I sat
next to her. Everyone knew she'd get
the part, so I couldn't wait to play

Judas and kiss her at rehearsals.

Fig. 9
ARA OSHAGAN
Hye Riders Motorcycle Club
Glendale, CA 2004

"The Hye (Armenian) Riders were established in Los Angeles over 25 years ago. 'Always where they are needed,' they have organized charity rides for the Armenian Bone Marrow Research Projects and assisted the needy in the community with donations and deliveries. The Hye Riders gather every Sunday to ride around town."

Christmas 2023 was very special. This photo in the exhibition prompted the Hye Riders to donate a truckload of new toys to the UCLA Mattel Children's Hospital as a gesture of community outreach and gratitude.

Fig. 10

ARA OSHAGAN

Santa Monica Boulevard
East Hollywood, Little
Armenia, CA, 2003

"The two store owners have commissioned their store signs, in Armenian, from the same sign maker: to the left is the shop of the tombstone carver, to the right that of the barber. The only clue that the stores are located in the U.S. is the (323) Hollywood area code."

Writer's Block at Father's Grocery Store

By SHAHÉ MANKERIAN

Coarse coffee grinds took the color
of Medusa's hair. A pound of garbanzo

weighed less than Nabokov's Lolita.
A bag of pita felt softer than Juliet's

pillow before suicidal Romeo. I wrote
countless villanelles on paper bags

before stuffing them with cans of dolma,
bottled rose water, and pouches

of Aleppo pepper. I thought I saw
the Karamazov Brothers tasting Kalamata

olives. Sometimes I sat on cardboard
boxes full of fava beans and daydreamed

about Anne Sexton. I couldn't write
because Father called me back to work.

Madame Bovary wanted two pounds
of French ham sliced thinner than lined paper.

Fig. 11
ARA OSHAGAN
Birth
Stepanakert, Artsakh, 2002

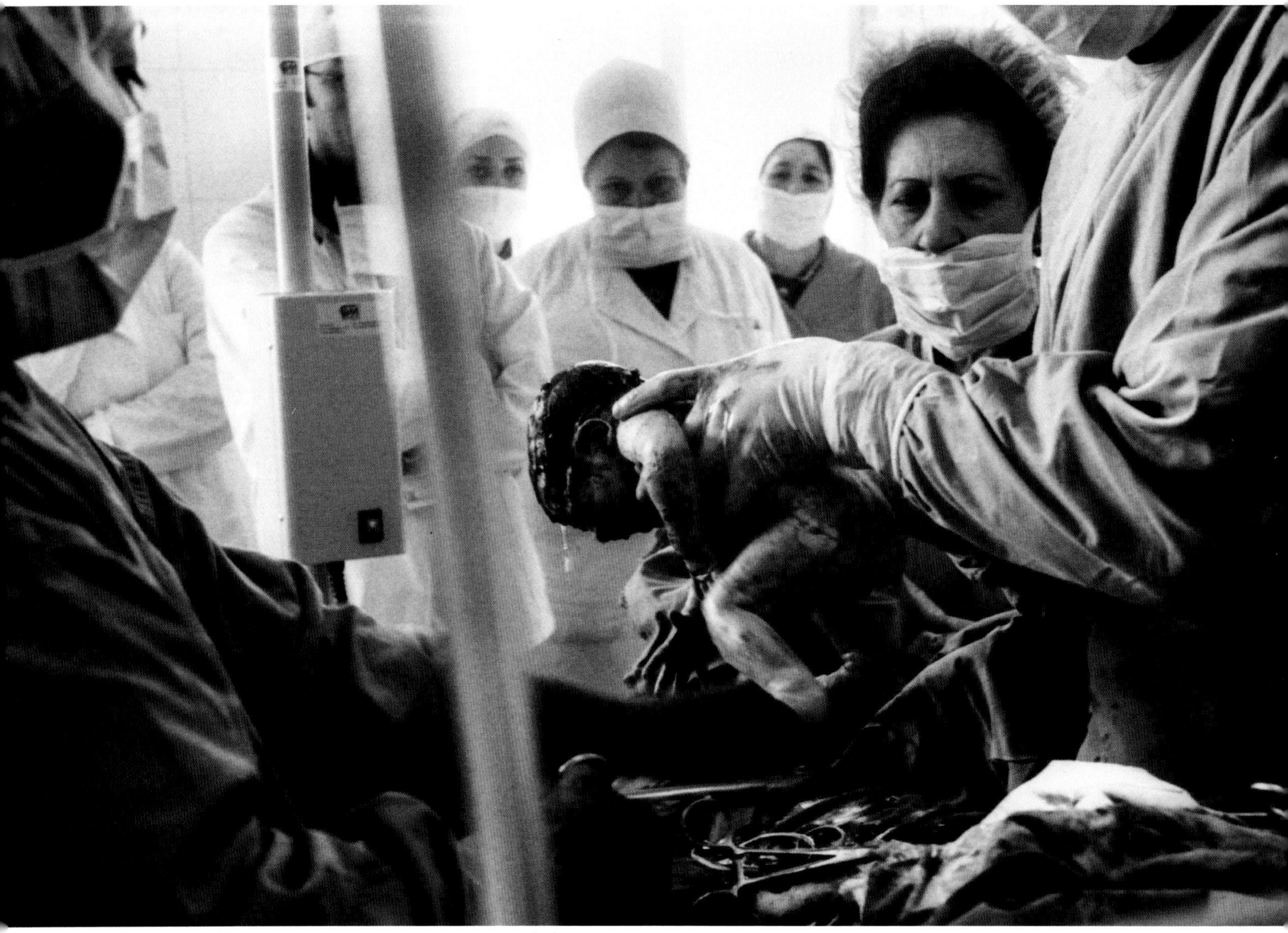

Where I Was Born

BY SHAHÉ MANKERIAN

Twenty years later, we went back to Beirut
and stood in front of CMC Hospital
for a photograph. We couldn't go inside.

During the war, it burned down,
not because of misguided bombs,
but because a doctor set himself on fire

after they wheeled his dead wife
into the Emergency. Years later, hollyhock
bushes and wild fig trees covered the pink

and black walls of the entrance.
Militiamen had posted pictures of martyrs
on the crooked wall that separated

the sidewalk from the front lawn.
The statue of Virgin Mary with broken
hands cried near a dehydrated water fountain.

Fig. 12
ARA OSHAGAN
Christening
Gantzasar Monastery
(13th century), Vank Village,
Artsakh, 2006 ©Ara Oshagan

"Der Hovaness, the priest at Gantzasar monastery, took up arms to defend his church and land during the first Artsakh war in the early 1990s."

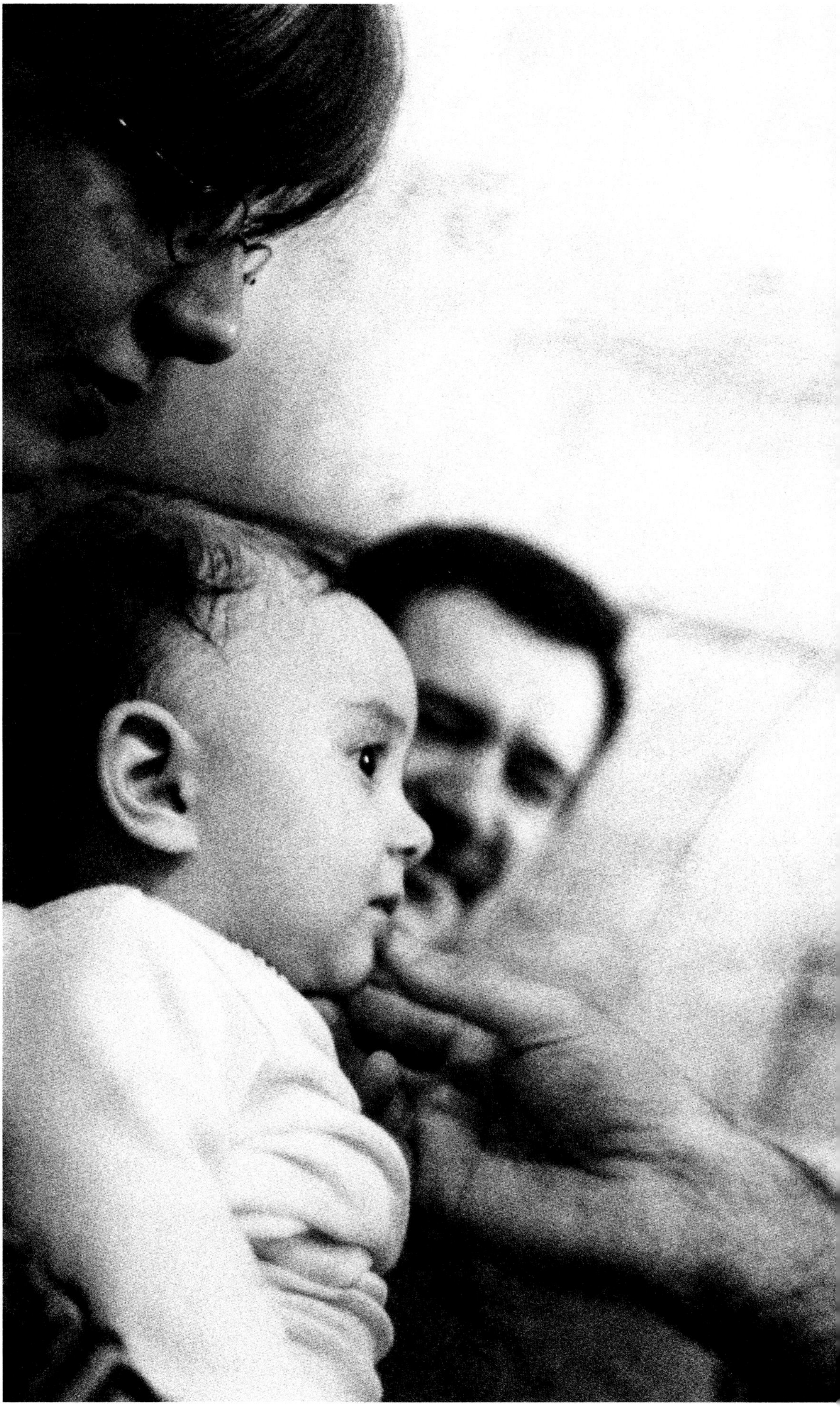

R Like Rabbit

BY RAFFI JOE WARTANIAN

R like Rabbit
A as in Alpha
F as in Frank
F as in Frank
I like iguana

W like water
A as in alpha
R as in rabbit
T as in Thomas
A as in alpha
N as in Nancy
I as in iguana
A as in apple
N as in Nancy

Did you get that? No?
Let's try again.

R as in revisionist subjugation to this bullshit
A as in are you aware that every time this happens my otherness expands
F as in frankly I'm
F as in fucking tired of this ritual, but fine
I as in I acquiesce to the inescapable subjugation of this inauthentic performance

W as in why? What happens to me every time I go through this?
A as in autopilot; I'm not even thinking anymore, I'm just
R as in reciting my otherness
T like the foundation for subjugation
A as in acceptance for the rest of my life
N like no escape from the
I as in immigrant's burden, even in the homeland, generations of displacement
squeezing me into this performance of the palatable other
A as in this ritual renders my name an apology
N as in n = a thousand and one = the lifetime sample size quantity of occasions
when I must lay out the letters of my name
like a rug to wipe your tongue on

Fig. 13
SOSSI MADZOUNIAN
Prayers
October 2015
Haghardzin Monastery (13th century), Dilijan, Tavush Province, Armenia ©Sossi Madzounian

"Individuals go to church to light candles, sending their prayers to God. The community of these candles sends the voice of the people to Heaven."

Fig. 14
SOSSI MADZOUNIAN
Mother and Child, Christening of the first-born son, 2015
Noravank Monastery (13th century), Vayotz Dzor Province, Armenia

"This image reflects the centuries-old respect for motherhood. The young mother holding her first-born son symbolizes this continuity and emanates the blessing of ancestral spirits. The portrait also echoes the tradition of adorning the altar of all Armenian Apostolic churches with Mother Mary holding Baby Jesus."

Fig. 15
SOSSI MADZOUNIAN
Heavenly Light, Noravank Monastery (13th century), Surb Krikor Church (Saint Gregory), Vayotz Dzor Province, Armenia, 2015
©Courtesy of the Ralph Rinzler Folklife Archives and Collections. Center for Folklife and Heritage, Smithsonian Institution

"The heavenly light pouring in through the carved wooden door illuminates the khatchkars (cross-stones) honoring prominent leaders and the tombstones of the ancestors set into the floor."

Turkification in Istanbul

BY SHAHÉ MANKERIAN

The Byzantine gate to the underground
bathhouse looked steamy and calloused.

Before we used the rooster knocker, a towel
boy with trimmed whiskers held the door for us.

He pointed to the dwarf hidden behind the register.
I placed coins in her sweaty palm. *Are you Jewish?*

She asked in Turkish. *We're Armenians.*
My wife smiled. The boy placed madras robes

on the bench near our feet. *I'll take your shoes
and polish them.* More Turkish. He bowed

to remove my dusty wingtips.

*My grandmother
prayed in Armenian,* he whispered,
but took the words with her when she died.

Fig. 16
SOSSI MADZOUNIAN
Areni Cave, Areni Village, Vayotz Dzor Province, Armenia, 2015
©Courtesy of the Ralph Rinzler Folklife Archives and Collections. Center for Folklife and Heritage, Smithsonian Institution

Armenia is famous worldwide for its wines. In 2007, an international team of archaeologists led by Boris Gasparyan (IAE NAS RA, Armenia), Gregory Areshian (CIOA, UCLA), and Ron Pinhasi (University of Cork, Ireland) uncovered numerous storage jars and vessels during excavations at the Areni-1 Cave site in the Vayots Dzor province, southeastern Armenia. Organic residue analysis conducted by Hans Barnard (CIOA UCLA) showed that one of the large jars (karas, կարաս)—imbedded into the ground with a clay platform built around it—contained evidence of wine. This 6,100-year-old wine press is the oldest one preserved in the world. The excavation was sponsored by UCLA, the National Geographic, the Institute of Archaeology and Ethnography of the National Academy of Sciences of the Republic of Armenia (IAE NAS RA), and the University of Cork. The Smithsonian Folk Art division commissioned Sossi Madzounian to photo-document the site in 2018.

Fig. 17
SOSSI MADZOUNIAN
Areni-1 Cave wine jars, 2018

Fig. 18
SOSSI MADZOUNIAN
Labor of Love-Lunchtime
Vayotz Tzor, Armenia, 2015
©Courtesy of the Ralph Rinzler Folklife Archives and Collections. Center for Folklife and Heritage, Smithsonian Institution

"These hard-working grape harvesters are on their lunch break outside the Areni Caves. The joy, the conviviality, and the sharing of good food energizes their tenacity and work."

Պարտէզը

Րաֆֆի Վարդանեան

Հայկ Նահապէտին պարտէզէն դուրս
Լեզուս քաղեցի
Հօրս պարտէզին մէջ,
որպէսզի Ուժ տայ բնութեան,
Որովհետեւ հոգիս
լոռւթենէն ալ յուսահատ է :
Անյոյս է
Որպէս սփիւռք
Որպէս ինքնաօտար
Որպէս հոգի ու վկայ եւ
Աքսորի զաւակ:
Պատերազմ և ողբերգութիւն
Կը կոչուին այդ երես լզողները, Ու ծնողքս,
իրենց հաճոյքը կը պահեն
Մեծմօրս գրպանին մեջ:
يعني sabersiz, mon ami

Այս կեանքը բնական չէ
Որովհետեւ ան
Կը ծաղկի
Կմախքի մը կողէն
Այն գերեզմանատան մէջ
Ուր կը Ֆր-ֆրա Հովը - Թուրքիոյ,
Հայաստանի ապա, Ռուսաստանի հովը,
Ամերիկայի, Չինաստանի, Ուրուկուաի
հովը - Նահատակներուն հովը, Ջոհերուն,
Երգիչին և արհեստաւորին հովը:
Բերնէդ բրցուած լեզուն
ընկղմեցաւ
Մելանին մէջ
ուր կրցաւ
պատմական նիւթեր գրել:

Ծովափին աւազներուն վրայ
Դարերու ընթացքին
Տարիներով
Օրերով
Մրջիւններով,

Türkçe dilinde,
En français
باللغة العربية

ENGLISH TRANSLATION

The Garden

WRITTEN & TRANSLATED BY RAFFI JOE WARTANIAN
LUTHERVILLE, MD // 2010

Outside Haig Nahabed's garden
I buried my tongue
Inside my father's garden
To give nature strength
Because my soul
In silence has grown hopeless.
Hopeless
As a diasporan
As self-estranged
As a soul and witness and
Child of exile.
War and tragedy
Are the names we give to those face-lickers,
    And my parents,
keep their joy
In my grandmother's pocket.
I mean the impatient one, my love.

This life is unnatural
For it
Blooms
From a skeleton
In a cemetery
Where winds blow – from Giligia,
    then Armenia, Artsakh's wind,
    from America,
China, Uruguay's wind – the wind of the
founders, of victims, of artists, and
    the wind of roots.
The tongue plucked from your mouth
drowned
in ink
where it could
pen histories
on shoreline sands

For days
Months
Years
Centuries
For words

Fig. 19
SOSSI MADZOUNIAN
Blue Slippers
Semyonovka village,
Gegharkunik Province,
Armenia, October 2015
©Sossi Madzounian

"The slippers in the photograph belong to the mother of the mayor of the village, which was established in 1845 by Molokan settlers from Russia—the Russians who split from the Russian Orthodox Church in the 17th century, rejecting the icons and the role of the clergy. The basis of their worship is the reading and study of the Bible. There are around 3,000 Molokans in Armenia. Presently, the village of Semyonovka is inhabited mainly by Armenians."

Only One or Two People Could Enter at a Time

BY TINA DEMIRDJIAN

I stepped into the old minivan
parked on my street
faded baby blue
and chipped paint
in front of my new place
on Mildford Avenue
where I bought
Persian cucumbers,
tomatoes, and figs.

Our street
lined with old men
in gray suits
who carried
worry beads
behind their back
and wives
in flowered dresses
who walked beside them
stepped in and out
all day
carrying bags
of groceries
to make dinner
until sunset
slatted
the black-paved road
where everything
was language
of memory
and time.

Where are you from?
the old man asked,
leaned over
in his white cotton shirt
to fix the bins
in this tiny space.

"Queens" I answered.
The other small man
with a gold tooth
clicked his tongue
in disapproval.
"No! Where are you from?"

"New York," I answered
again in Armenian.
Their eyes narrowed,
and heads now at a slant.

So, I replied:
"Istanbul. Bolis."

They waited; the minivan
now silent.
One hand on the hip,
small eyes
now a bit shiny,
noses, long
and rounded
like my ancestors.

"Where is your family from?"

"Gesaria, my family is
    from Gesaria."

"Ah, now I know who
    you are,"
they said simultaneously,
    and smiled.

It was my ancestors
they were looking for.

Fig. 20
SOSSI MADZOUNIAN
Lavash Bread
Rind Village in Areni Region, Vayotz Dzor Province, Armenia, 2015
©Courtesy of the Ralph Rinzler Folklife Archives and Collections. Center for Folklife and Heritage, Smithsonian Institution

"Lavash is a flat bread made of three ingredients: wheat flour, salt, and water. It can also contain flax, oat bran, and whole wheat. Lavash has been an integral part of Armenian culture for millennia." In 2014, it was inscribed on the UNESCO Representative List of the Intangible Cultural Heritage of Humanity (9.COM.10.3).

I Want to Wrap Myself…

BY TINA DEMIRDJIAN

I want to wrap myself
in grape leaves

so you can taste
my grandmother's
cooking from New York
a world not far
from your
backdoor now
you smell me
simmering in the pot
waiting for your hands
to touch my skin
rolled to keep
the flavor
inside your mouth.

Fig. 21
SOSSI MADZOUNIAN
Pure Honey
Vayotz Dzor Province, Armenia, 2015

"Jars of pure golden honey sold at the Areni Wine Festival, Vayotz Dzor Province, in 2015. This honey has no additional ingredients, such as sugar. It contains only the blessings of the bees."

For Olives

BY ARMINÉ IKNADOSSIAN

In Greek mythology, olives were a gift to humankind by the goddess Athena.

They rained down from the trees during Santa Ana Winds.
My mother, every weekend, bed sheets ready in the trunk of her car,
drove to my high school, laid the sheets out under the trees,
shook the trees or simply gathered the fallen,

tossing them by the handful into plastic grocery bags.
Large jars filled with water, salt, vinegar, lemon, thyme, garlic.
Mother craved olives every day during her pregnancy.
I was born with an olive-shaped birthmark on my left calf.

Leave them brining for a week or two, the longer the sweeter.
Warm the pita over the burner. Sliced tomato,
fresh mint from the side garden. Dirt under nails.
Pits spit into palms, spoons, napkins. Wrinkled black Greek ones,

Turkish green, Kalamata, Mission. A clutch of green onions
next to the mint, a small dish for the pits. A pit in the stomach
grows a tree. A tree is a home. Rain fed, dirt fed, sun fed.
A woman feeds her family with what she gathers in her arms.

My family ate them after every meal, crushed them into paste,
made whole meals out of them when meat was scarce. Olives keep well.

In the trunk of my mother's car, you will always find:
a jar of olives, a change of clothes, running shoes.

Fig. 22
SOSSI MADZOUNIAN
Meeting of the Souls
Haghartzin Monastery
(13 century) Dilijan, Tavush
Province, October 2015
©Sossi Madzounian

"The bridge connecting the three crosses on the church domes stands for the strength of the Armenian people and their faith, which has acted as a community-binding glue, empowering them at home and in diaspora. When I saw this scenery, I realized how tight and close the faith is. Nothing can break the faith in us. The strength of the structure that is standing tall portrays the Armenian people. It is our faith that has held us together, moved us forward, and helped us procreate for centuries."

Fig. 23

SOSSI MADZOUNIAN
Harout and his books
Hollywood, Little Armenia, CA, 1985 ©Sossi Madzounian

"Abril ('to live' and 'April' in Armenian) Bookstore opened its doors in April 1977. The intention of its proprietor, Harout Yeretzian, was to establish a community center and to encourage political, cultural, and economic discussions of current events through books. Today, the bookstore remains a vibrant gathering place in the Armenian neighborhood of Glendale, CA."

Our Customs

BY ARMINÉ IKNADOSSIAN

Eat boiled wheat and pomegranate seeds to celebrate a baby's new tooth.
Announce *sweet bath water* to a newly bathed person,
and they must give you their clean cheek to kiss.

This is lucky and good. This makes God happy.
Read your fortune in the dark maps left behind in coffee cups,
and believe it, but don't bet on it.

Name your daughter or son Revenge. This is not a metaphor.
This means they will put fear into their enemies,
the devil and their children.

Throw a raw egg at the tire of a brand new car,
but don't wash it off for that will cause a tragic accident;
it happened to my uncle.

When you announce travel plans, end with *God willing*,
and always follow praise with a criticism,
especially with those you love the most.
If your palms itch, this is a sign of money coming to you.
This is not a rash but an invitation by God
to buy a lottery ticket.

Blue glass eyes ward off evil so hang one from your rearview mirror
and pin it on a newborn baby.
If they break, a tragedy has been avoided.

And when you spot a new moon, laugh out loud.
That's God smiling at you,
and it would be rude to not smile back.

Fig. 24
SOSSI MADZOUNIAN
Spirits in Action
Noravank Monastery (13th century), Vayotz Dzor Province, Armenia, October 2015

"The door is always open for the spirits and the light to come in. They are in the cemetery in the monastery's courtyard. They surround the structure, the monks, the people of the neighboring villages and town, and keep them under constant protection. These vigilant spirits protect the land and its inhabitants from all visible and invisible harm."

Mama's Dream

BY RAFFI JOE WARTANIAN

My mother told my grandmother and me
About a dream she had
Last night.

Her deceased father
Visited
And said,
"Have you forgotten me?"

"No, I didn't,"
My mother protested,
In her dream.

My mother is silent.

"What happened next," I ask.
"That's it," she says with a shrug.

Then my grandmother inquires,
"Did he ask about me?"

Meg

BY TINA DEMIRDJIAN

On mornings the wind
brings dead leaves
from trees to the ground

the Santa Ana's
fierce and unforgiving
dictate their fate

while Meg sweeps the fallen

her 90-year-old bones
thin as a yellowed leaf
wisp the leaves like a broom
around the curve

where two soldiers
once came long ago
and knocked on her door

We are sorry to inform you
your son has died at war

and the letter in their hands trembled:

the way the leaves
trembled in the wind
before Meg swept them
after each storm.

She'd gather them into piles
like words on a page
she'd try to make sense of:

the word war she'd rid of
into the dustpan first
and swerve the broom
around the curve to find
the word died
and let it rest for a while.

The word son she'd sweep
closer to her to keep an eye on
like a little boy at her side
until she was done
until all was swept away

she'd pick him up

and give him back to the wind
like news that travels in silence.

Fig. 25
ARA MGRDICHIAN
Convergence
Noravank Monastery (13th century),
Vayotz Tsor Province,
Armenia, 2018
©Ara Mgrdichian

"Sacred geometric architecture merges with beyond sacred ancient landscapes and skyscapes. Pointed domes pierce ominous, yet sheltering skies, producing transcendence."

The New World

BY ARTHUR KAYZAKIAN

In fourth grade we played a board game
for Thanksgiving.
My classmates were thrilled to ration
food and clothing, trading skin
for spear and rifle.
I was not interested in expansion.
I was more into Stephanie's hair,
how at her scalp it was light
but darkened on the way down,
darkened to the color of rope.
Her eyes lit up when our wagon
moved across the mountains.
She was willing to barter away
our horses for land.
We named our group The Pioneers.
On our map we marked a big red x
across a region of grayed out hills.
"This is where we will live" she said.
But I wondered where we would die?
Who wants to name our grave site? I said.
When it came to cemeteries, no one answered.

Fig. 26
ARA MGRDICHIAN
Resolve
Ornate government building, Republic Square, Yerevan, Armenia, 2018

"Tufa stone, volcanic and still alight with intricate lace-like carvings and bas-reliefs, telling millennial stories along social realist roads and proclamations of freedom. Governments change, the ornate stone remains resolute, in resolve. It survives like the people who carved the stories of their molten souls into the eternal rock."

Fig. 27

ARA MGRDICHIAN

North by Northwest

Northern Avenue, Yerevan, Armenia, 2018

"The physical correlative of Yerevan's original city planner/ architect Tamanyan's extended vision of the city, Northern Avenue becomes another ray of light in a sun-shaped circularity radiating outward past itself toward the sacred mountain, Ararat, just out of reach."

"DISCO DATEV," 2023

TABLATURE MUSICAL NOTATION OF AN ORIGINAL COMPOSITION BY RAFFI JOE WARTANIAN FOR HIS SON DATEV

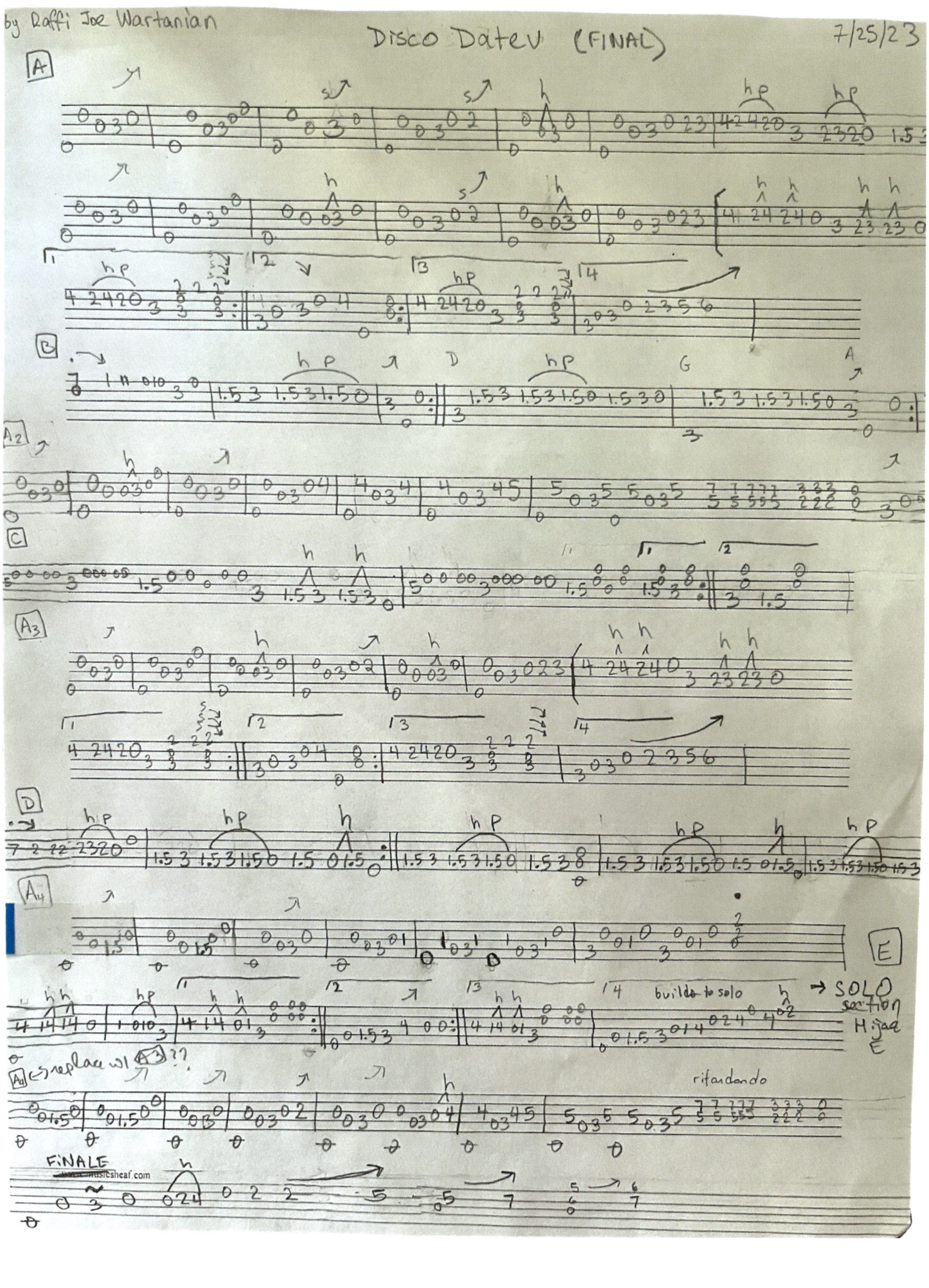

Fig. 28
ARA MGRDICHIAN
Hand in Hand
Orran Center for socially vulnerable children and families, Yerevan, Armenia, 2018 ©Ara Mgrdichian

"Caring for orphans and street kids in a land built and beautified by the orphans of genocide and refugees, as they find solace and support in a real home and homeland—adopted for some, but forever real."

Fig. 29
ARA MGRDICHIAN
Quo Vadis?
Sister cities signpost,
City Hall, Los Angeles, CA,
2016 ©Ara Mgrdichian

"The Angels (Los Angeles) have many sisters, a diverse family strewn, but all coming together, here, in the diaspora of diasporas. Can you go home if you're already (t)here?"

Fig. 30
ARA MGRDICHIAN
Beautiful Exile
110 North/10 East freeway interchange, Los Angeles, CA, 2016 ©Ara Mgrdichian

"Becoming indigenous in a foreign place, home in this case is never homeland. Displacement is real and volumetric in space, time, and mind."

Exiled: Los Angeles

BY ARTHUR KAYZAKIAN

We fled from green oil tanks and the scent of chemicals,
from fire bluster and windows rattled by gunfire.

We fled to make poems out of cemeteries
and write prose out of psalms.

Here, our windows are stained with promise.
Our prayers are made of glass.

From a confiscated garden infested with guards,
we fled to an army of daffodils.

We fled and we fled from Allah
burning in the trees, from gutted staircases

and swollen buildings sinking to the sand.
We fled from the parade of sirens.

Here, at night, dogs bark in the junkyard.
Our hands up against the wall,

we have been taught we die without one another.
What do we know of love?

Kitchen in Pasadena

ARMINÉ IKNADOSSIAN

Mother stirs the soup.
Says she smells the Mediterranean.

A Monarch butterfly appears from behind dish rack
on her way to Mexico or San Simeon.

Glides from faucet to shoulder to ladle.
Together, they listen to the bubbling of the ocean.

Fig. 31
ARA MGRDICHIAN
Mgrdoutioune
Arpa and Charlie Rose Hachadourian, baptism, Saint Mary's Armenian Church, Glendale, CA, 2015

"Baptisms of fire and water from thousands of years and thousands of miles to the here and now and well beyond... Love, Faith, and Hope intoned perfectly in a conscious mouth or in the inconsolable affirmation of an infant's cry—the message is clear to all far and near: '...we are here, we are here, we are here...alight, alive, in light...'"

My Name

BY SHAHÉ MANKERIAN

To the American ear
Shahé is a mistake.
It's a crazy consonant
malfunction, alphabetic
disorder. The boys at Starbucks
want to relabel me: "Shane,
your coffee's ready!"
"Sean, non-fat latte, extra foam."
It's no use correcting them,
because in their world I am
wrong and they're right.
In their world Armenian is
a typo, it should be American.
Computers often recognize me
as a verb: Shake, shave, share-
Depends on who wants to play
Scrabble with me that day.
My name is Shahé;
Shale sounds nice,
but it's not my name.
In Turkish, "Shash" means
cross-eyed peasant.
It's not my name.
Shat is the past
tense of shit.
It's not my name.
Shawe almost sounds
like a playwright.
Shaqe sounds like a basketball player.
Shame,
shame,
shame,
not my name.
My name is Shahé.
It has a powerful connotation of the Shah,
and a simple "héh" like a whisper,
like a sigh on a cold winter day,
like the end of a poem.

Fig. 32
ARA MGRDICHIAN
Fight the Power
Protest against the Turkish genocide of Armenians, Wilshire Boulevard, Los Angeles, CA, 2015
©Ara Mgrdichian

"Progeny of Armenian genocide survivors, forever alive, marching not in death march deserts, but on smooth American streets, in an adopted exile home, at the behest of millions of murdered ancestors. The world still turns a blind eye, supporting makers of genocide still ongoing, as the perpetrators try to erase Armenia, Armenians, and their culture—home, homeland, and diaspora—from memory and this earth."

Cookie Monster's Genocide

BY RAFFI JOE WARTANIAN

Cookie Monster came for the sweets
He stayed for the genocide
Superman saw the slaughter
In the name of the father, the son, and the holy
Three percent interest rates
If you sign up in the next three days
Terms and conditions apply
We remember our fallen ancestors
We remember the new smartphone
We demand recognition for the crimes
We demand the new
Superman demands pay from tourists for the photo op
Atop extracted souls' indigenous roots
We prey upon this sacrament
Industrialized morality morphing essence into performance
Unless essence is the performance
And morality is the mask
What remains, then, is the empty mirror, the forgotten promise,
And a flock of rats feasting on Cookie Monster's memory cortex

Fig. 33
ARA MGRDICHIAN
The Displacing Moment
Man at a photo exhibition in downtown Los Angeles, 2019
©Ara Mgrdichian

"Being in one place, living one reality and feeling, living—another, strikes at the core of the issue of exile and displacement. The variegation of images corresponds directly to the variegation of experiences of living in exile. Being in one place, which may be your home, but viewing and feeling other places that may be equally, if not more, indigenous is a dichotomy—or polyvalence, rather—that leads to a longing for both where you are and where you aren't, evoking a specificity while masking the absence of an intangible or lost other(ness), a reality gone awry."

War-torn

ARMINÉ IKNADOSSIAN

It is mid-summer, and watermelons are left to cool in the streams.
Ladies lean out their windows,

braid gossip between the crippled cousin of Satan,
Christ wearing a red sash like a beauty queen.

All these fallen apples we have eaten
in this tired age of our own curiosity.

The architecture of ritual is an exercise in futility.
Think of a room you have not bled in.

Think of the seedling, the unrelenting, the turning.
The beast is churning in the season of blood.

Credo in unum Deum is a dream
you deconstruct over breakfast.

But no commonplace prayers today,
no more sleepwalking towards the volcano.

We have applied the gauze, we have defined
where we come from – a changing question.

A new shadow is here, and that formal feeling
sleeps in the eaves, the music of guilt and silence.

I come from a family of missing paintings

ARTHUR KAYZAKIAN

I come from a family of Iranian art lovers.

I'm kidding. I come from a family of
redacted art, by which I mean we hold
back what we say.

In the tower of my birth, my mother was sick.
The art of survival on a torrid war-torn block.

I was born in the year of the snake.
Some mistake my creativity for a bite.

My mother's cousin could pay off our debts.
He rarely attends holiday dinners, but we feel
his electrons circulating through his chair.

My body is a toe tag for my name.

My mother says everything is about money—
even the sky leased the moon to the night.

I am fond of Batman. His vulnerability. The
way he gets his ass kicked in dark alleys that
smell of smoke and gutter water.

Maybe there is an empty room glowing
in the back of my eye.

The men in my family have a sense
of departure written on their faces.

Fun fact: The last episode of the Dark
Knight series blared on our television when
the Ayatolla dragged our paintings out of
the house.

There have been rumors that my mom's side
of the family drinks blood to replace their
thirst for money.

The great Arshile Gorky's last words should
have been: My only regret is my inability to
paint the dreams trapped in my arm.

My body grows jealous of my name with each
passing year. My name does not age. My war
name. My name was given a certificate from
the state that my body cannot afford.

Tell me. Why does talking to my uncle
feel like drinking with my shadow?

Fun fact: every painting is charged with war
then sentenced to a life of hanging.

To describe my father, I will need the weight
of a missing person.

Dear God: what if the snake is a year and not
the blame for your poor design?

My doctor looks puzzled. She said my brain
scan shows an empty gallery of walls stained
with stolen art.

My body carries the charge of a missing
painting. A chamber for tourists. A scar on
a wall after confiscation.

Dear officer. I am not vicious. I swear it.
My teeth may be sharp, but I am as innocu-
ous as the cousin of a fly wing.

The pacing of footsteps thumping from my
ceiling denotes that men in my family are
bloodthirsty poltergeists.

Dear Government and Empire of the State:
In the mirror, my year is stuck to my skin,
the way your language hooked its way into
my mouth.

Just give me a window, so I can measure the
chemical change in the air after a body slips
through it.

I'm kidding. The men in my family are
bloodthirsty business owners who eat
poltergeists on their lunch breaks.

Fig. 34
ARA MGRDICHIAN
Eternity
Monument Obelisk,
Yerevan, Armenia, 2018

"Ancient Armenian eternity symbol bas-relief on a 65-meter obelisk located on the highest hill overlooking Yerevan. The Armenian eternity symbol can be traced back millennia, symbolizing fecundity, flux, and the ever-present life-force of the sun."

Infinity of a Small Space

TINA DEMIRDJIAN

Light grows scarcer as the afternoon drifts;
forms shadows on books tightly fit onto shelves
like mumbo jumbo words in a poem I write
no spaces in between to breathe;
so I inhale to learn how to remember;
exhale to know how to live in tight quarters.
What will it take to make me stay a while?

We root ourselves unknowingly in what is hidden,
moments smashed into sentences;
traces of memory: nothing is chronological:
the drift of light from the sun in the yellow vase;
the pink rose blossoming on the quiet table,
the infant drinking milk who stops to look up
to meet mother's eyes for the first time.

How does something mean everything?

How do we trace our lives back and forth?

How do voices accumulate behind walls?

How do we bend our ear to hear a whisper?

How do we become someone we weren't before?

Fig. 35
ARA MGRDICHIAN
Remain in Light
Gandzasar Monastery
(13th century)
Vank, Artsakh, 2018

"Armenian priest performing a liturgical purifying ritual, as has been done for centuries, burning myrrh and frankincense in a holy censer in front of this altar under which, it is said, is buried the head of John the Baptist and other holy relics, moved and enshrined therein (during the Crusades) to ensure they would never be destroyed by ill-intentioned marauders."

Curator's Photo Album

Fig. 36
ARA MGRDICHIAN
Illuminated, 2019
Charlie Hachadourian,
Sculptor, Pasadena, CA

A Line Breaks like Twilight

TINA DEMIRDJIAN

Words peel off each sentence
as if night is about to fall
and I fit in like a line break;

imaginary and incandescent
a trail that leads me into twilight;
in between marsh lands
before the sun rises

while the wind blows a passageway;
a tunnel, a pause, a breath
the time before I knew you
before I knew myself

before I knew our daughter
would need to go away
in order to be whole,
before you and I were a poem

uncertain of its ending.

Fig. 37
ARA MGRDICHIAN
Kookla and Charlie Rose, 2016
Hachadourian Residence,
Pasadena, CA

Fig. 38
ARA OSHAGAN
Anahid, incarcerated at
Los Angeles Central Juvenile
Hall, Los Angeles, 2002

Rose of Sharon

ARMINÉ IKNADOSSIAN

She sticks her red tongue out to God,
fed up with his promises and tinted glasses.
He is a mendacious flatterer,
cloud of gathering sextons, soul-monger.

She opens her face to him
but all he offers are his coattails,
his severance package, his adamantine farce.
Lover boy, charlatan, beautiful executioner.

She nudges closer, her velveteen skin
wanting his fake valentine,
his infinite jest, daddy in a yew tree,
edge of love, sultan of lost sheep.

And afterwards, he is already looking
for his Moleskine and Gauloises,
already standing in the doorway,
black leather, white teeth,
handsome conqueror, filthy beast.

Fig. 39
ARA MGRDICHIAN,
Anahid Redux, 2019
Concrete cast rendering of Anahid, Armenian goddess of fertility and healing, wisdom and water. Charlie Hachadourian's backyard studio, Pasadena, CA

Vitiligo

SHAHÉ MANKERIAN

Pale patches appeared on grandmother's feet
during the death march from Arapkir to Aleppo.

She wore wool socks for the rest of her life.
After marriage, she lost pigmentation on her hands.

She couldn't hide those. I tended to stare at the lesions
as she sifted through lentils for rocks and pebbles.

Maybe her discolored hands veiled the secret map
of her tormented underworld. Sometimes I traced

the borders when I napped next to her in the afternoons.
"Armenians are the lepers of the world," she'd mumble

in her sleep and shift to face the wall against her bed.

Fig. 40
SOSSI MADZOUNIAN
Mamig (grandma) has seen a lot in her lifetime, but today, her pride and joy is her son, the Mayor of Semyonovka.

History of Forgetfulness

SHAHÉ MANKERIAN

She might finally forget
my name when she's dicing
onions on a chopping block.

For now, Mother can't pinpoint
my daughter's birthday; she recites
random months like, January

and August, until I remind her
it's in July. She forgets to swallow
her blood pressure pills,

so she leaves church early.
After she calms her heart, she drinks
Turkish coffee. No one knows

why she clips coupons for Campbell's
tomato soup. She makes illegal
U-turns just to make sure the burner

under the pressure cooker is off.
She can't sleep at night
because when she closes her eyes,

she remembers everything.

Fig. 41
ARA MGRDICHIAN
Unger..., 2014
Papken Sassouni, Sassouni Residence, Hollywood Hills, Los Angeles, CA

Fig. 42
ARA OSHAGAN
Armenian Power gang member, Ironwood State Prison, Blithe, CA, 2004
©Ara Oshagan

There Is No Word for This Name

ARTHUR KAYZAKIAN

Mother said
it looks like a stain from a bracelet
    around the wrist.

A grapple phantom.

A sort of hue that surfaces when one
    is pulled through the door.

It is the astronomy of the hand
    best seen through cause and effect
mother said.

She was scientific about it, touching
    the solar system
pulsing around her eye.

When I ask you to name it,
you parade the garden with ghosts
    on your tongue

calling out to the prisoners who slipped
    through the fences—
the part history leaves out.

It used to mean sitting in the balcony,
    moon split in half.

How this was a mirror planet—
that half of the world does not exist.
You left that part out, didn't you?

That you reside in the misplaced side
    of the moon.

Fine, I believe you.

You named it the residue of night falling on a
    garland of dark petals,
steam rising from a black teacup

with your lips smudged on the rim on the last
    day you took a sip.

Since you've been gone,
I've tried to name every bird perched
    on the branches.

I need to know what flies out
    of the holes in our lives.

I had to read it twice.
My name has a wavy bounce.

Under the glow of a light bulb, it glimmers off
    government documents, sits next
to a polygraphed sticker of an eagle

and the well-rested signature of the state,

which appears longer with more vowels
    and loops.

When I read it the second time, it feels like a
    transaction
running through me.

Careful not to leave my fingerprints behind,
I hold the certificate with gloves.

And in the back of my head,
from somewhere in the past, lingers

the crypto-biotic sound of my mother
    saying my name

Fig. 43
SOSSI MADZOUNIAN
Mrs. Gohar, the personification of hospitability, serves the guests at her Airbnb with love and a generous smile.
©Sossi Madzounian

Oranges from the Bosphorus

TINA DEMIRDJIAN

She fed me oranges and my worries went
away
on the road from the Bosphorus
I spit the seeds out the window
of the small white car
speeding down the mountain
at fifteen I planted my memory
there on the dirt road
and found the beginning of where
my skin was born
on the hands of all my grandmothers

waving to me on that dirt road;
shouting their stories in the wind
so I can hear their echo
even in the speeding car,
and carry voices in my pocket
eating oranges
laughing and telling jokes
in another language,
and smiling each time

I see an old woman reminding me
of all my grandmothers
and all their sad eyes staring
at me, watching me leave
the land where they were born;
hoping I take a piece of them
with me to remember when I am old.

Fig. 44
SOSSI MADZOUNIAN
Young dancers in the traditional Armenian folkloric costumes in Rind village, Areni Wine Festival, Vayotz Dzor Province, October 2015

Fig. 45
ARA OSHAGAN
Christening, St. Garabed
Armenian Apostolic Church,
Little Armenia, East
Hollywood, CA, 2002

Fig. 46
ARA OSHAGAN
Martial arts practice, Olymp Studio, Glendale, 2002

Fig. 47
ARA MGRDICHIAN
Arils in Hand, Passing on the Light, 2013
Armenian woman at home, Los Angeles, CA

1974

ARMINÉ IKNADOSSIAN

I was born from the mouth
of Hecate and Hera, a thin red thread
attaching our throats

each mouth a crack of thunder
a limping childhood
arrested development

my seaside suicide
was born nine months after me
baptized in holy debris and decadence,

a country too small to matter
my left heel dipped in Mercury and Molotov cocktail
my right heel stained by the juice of 1.5 million pomegranates

Contributors

GASSIA ARMENIAN is a curator and research associate at the Fowler Museum at UCLA, where she conducts collections and database research to facilitate curatorial and scholarly efforts and manages various aspects of planning and organizing exhibitions. She curated Fowler exhibitions: *Janyak: Armenian Art of Knots and Loops* and *Remain In Light: Visions of Homeland and Diaspora*. In 2023, both received recognition from the Armenian Academy of Sciences, Diaspora Division, and the Sardarapat Museum of Ethnography in the Republic of Armenia. The exhibition *Joli! Fancy Masquerade from Sierra Leone* (2016–2017), curated by Armenian, was the first to feature an interactive CT scan on an iPad in the gallery. Currently, she is the in-house curator of *Mountain Spirits*, which highlights the history, customs, and beliefs of the Ifugao people of the North Luzon Peninsula of the Philippines. Additionally, she is developing an exhibition linking global artists to local communities. Armenian liaises with domestic and international institutional and private lenders to the museum. She has helped to mount many Fowler exhibitions, including: *Striking Iron: the Art of African Blacksmiths* (2018); *From X to Why: A Museum Takes Shape* (2013–14), *World Arts/Local Lives: The Collections of the Fowler Museum at UCLA* (2014); *Secrets d'Ivoire: L'art des Lega d'Afrique central* (Fowler traveling exhibition at the Musée du quai Branly, Paris, 2013); *Central Nigeria Unmasked: Arts of the Benue River Valley* (2012); *Architecture of the Veil: An Installation by Samta Benyahia* (2007); *A Saint in the City: Sufi Arts of Urban Senegal* (2003). Prior to the Fowler, Armenian was a consultant-project coordinator at the U.S. Agency for International Development—for Junior Achievement of Armenia, where she developed and implemented civics-education training programs and teaching methodologies for principals and teachers from the Republic of Armenia in the United States and Armenia. In addition, Armenian has taught world cultures and history at the Ferrahian Armenian School, Encino, CA.

TINA DEMIRDJIAN is a poet who has taught poetry in Los Angeles schools, museums, libraries, and businesses for more than 30 years. She is also a culture bearer, preserving Armenian traditions through her writing practice, art education, and founding and co-directing the Armenian Dress & Textile Project. She is the author of the poetry collection *Imprint*, and her work is anthologized in *Birthmark: A Bilingual Anthology of Armenian-American Poetry*. Her work has appeared in the *Armenian Poetry Project, Moria, High Performance, Texas Observer*, and the *Midwest Poetry Review*. She has performed her poetry throughout Los Angeles and at The Bowery in New York. A recent finalist for the Arts & Letters Rumi Prize, she is the recipient of grants from the Department of Cultural Affairs, the Durfee Foundation, and California Council for the Humanities. She is currently on the Board of Brand Library & Art Center, where she also co-facilitates ARTful Conversations.

ARMINÉ IKNADOSSIAN was born in Beirut, Lebanon. Her family fled to California when she was four years old to escape the civil war. After graduating from UCLA, she earned an M.F.A. in creative writing at Antioch University. She is the author of *All That Wasted Fruit* (Main Street Rag), and her work has appeared in *XLA Anthology, Whale Road Review, Southern Florida Poetry Journal, MacQueen's Quarterly*, and *The American Journal of Poetry*. She has received fellowships from Idyllwild Arts, the Los Angeles Writing Project, and Otis College of Art and Design. Recently, Iknadossian's poems were featured in *XLA Poets Anthology* (Hinchas Press) along with nine other women of color who represent Los Angeles's diversity. Project 1521 is another one of her passion endeavors. A collaboration between artist Sandy Rodriguez, writer/KPCC reporter Adolfo Guzman-Lopez, and six other local artists, writers, and scholars, it was inspired by Indigenous perspectives on the Spanish invasion. The project seeks to generate visual and literary works as acts of resistance.

ARTHUR KAYZAKIAN is the winner of the 2021 inaugural Black Lawrence Immigrant Writing Series award for his collection, *The Book of Redacted Paintings*, which was also selected as a finalist for the 2021 Philip Levine Prize for Poetry. He is the recipient of a 2023 creative writing fellowship from the National Endowment for the Arts; the winner of the Prairie Schooner Strousse award; and of the Open Chapbook Competition for his collection *My Burning City*. He serves as the poetry chair for the International Armenian Literary Alliance. His work has appeared in several publications, including: *The Adroit Journal, Portland Review, Chicago Review, Cincinnati Review, The Southern Review, Michigan Quarterly Review*, and *Witness Magazine*.

SOSSI MADZOUNIAN is a Los Angeles-based fine art photographer with a background in commercial photography, having studied at the Art Center College of Design in Pasadena. After a successful career in that field, she shifted her focus to fine art, capturing the essence of unheeded subjects and transforming them into compelling visual narratives. Her work has been exhibited in numerous solo and group shows, including at the Multiverse Art Gallery at San Francisco City Hall, Downtown LA // IRL, Ten Women Gallery in Santa Monica, and the Chania International Photo Festival in Crete, Greece. Madzounian's photography has been featured in prestigious publications, such as APA's *Off the Clock* and Communication Arts' *Photography Annual 62*. She has also been recognized by IPA, LensCulture, and Lucie Foundation. Her artistic contributions extend to set designs for shows like *Ray Donovan, Bosch House*, and *Big Brother*. She has also collaborated with the Smithsonian Institute on the folklore project My Armenia: her work was showcased at the Smithsonian Summer Festival. Most recently, her photography was featured in the *Lily Vorperian Marash Embroidery* publication, the Fowler Museum's *Remain in Light: Visions of Homeland and Diaspora* exhibition, the Armenian Arts Gallery in Glendale, and The Collective Realty/Gallery in West Hollywood. With a discerning eye and an unblemished approach to life, Madzounian continues to find inspiration in the beauty of everyday subjects, transforming them into profound artistic expressions.

SHAHÉ MANKERIAN is the principal of St. Gregory Hovsepian School in Pasadena, CA, and the director of mentorship at the International Armenian Literary Alliance. He previously served as co-director of the Los Angeles Writing Project and is a recipient of the Los Angeles Music Center's BRAVO Award for innovation in arts education. Mankerian's debut poetry collection, *History of Forgetfulness*, was published in 2021 by Fly on the Wall Press (UK), listed as a semifinalist for the Khayrallah Prize, and a finalist for the Bibby First Book Competition, the Crab Orchard Poetry Open Competition, the Julie Suk Award, the Quercus Review Press Poetry Book Award, and the White Pine Press Poetry Prize.

ARA MGRDICHIAN is a writer, artist, and counselor whose work—creative, analytic, and therapeutic—often deals with issues of epigenetics, transgenerational justice, trauma, and memory. He has lived the greater part of his life in the Los Angeles area, with three years in the Republic of Armenia (1990–93) and extended stays in Artsakh. He has worked as a teacher, violence prevention specialist, journalist, and essayist; published poetry and prose; and provided curatorial writing and direction for arts and educational projects. Mgrdichian was a founding member of *Exile* biweekly; his work has been included in anthology with noteworthy authors, including Donald Freed, Harold Pinter, and A.J. Langguth; and featured in the *Anthology of Armenian Poets*. He is the voice of William Saroyan in Lusin Dink's full-length film *Saroyanland*. Mgrdichian's photographs were featured in the *Remain in Light: Visions of Homeland and Diaspora* at the Fowler Museum. He has received a variety of private and public-sector awards for his work with young people, schools, and the community at large. He is currently developing a variety of projects, some collaborative, featuring his analytic, photographic, and poetic efforts.

ARA OSHAGAN is a diasporic trans-disciplinary artist, curator, and cultural worker whose practice explores collective and personal histories of dispossession, legacies of violence, identity, colonial afterlives, and (un)imagined futures. His curatorial work engenders dialogue and discourse between diverse cultural and diasporic artistic communities. Oshagan works in photography, film, collage, installation, book arts, public art, and monuments. He has published four books of photography: *Fatherland* (Powerhouse, 2010), *Mirror* (self-published, 2016), *displaced* (Kehrer Verlag, 2022), and *A Poor Imitation of Death* (Daylight, 2024). Oshagan has presented his work at the Annenberg Space for Photography, International Center of Photography in NY, Meta headquarters in Seoul, Korea, and TedX Yerevan. He has participated in solo exhibitions in Los Angeles, New York, Morocco, and South Korea, as well as in multiple group shows. His work has been reviewed and featured in *Art Papers, Hyperallergic, LA Times, LA Weekly*, NPR's Morning Edition, *Virginia Quarterly Review, Artillery Mag, and Mother Jones*, among others. He has been designated as one of "100 Leading Global Thinkers" by *Foreign Policy* magazine and a "Cultural Trailblazer" by the Los Angeles Department of Cultural Affairs. Oshagan's work is in the permanent collection of Craft Contemporary Museum, Armenian Museum of America, Stockton University Art Gallery, the Southeast Museum of Photography, Los Angeles Municipal Art Gallery, Pasadena Armory Center for the Arts, the Downey Museum of Art, and MOMA in Armenia. Oshagan is an Artist-in-Residence at the 18th Street Art Center in Santa Monica and a curator at ReflectSpace Gallery in the City of Glendale.

RAFFI JOE WARTANIAN is a writer, musician, and educator who teaches writing at UCLA and currently serves as the inaugural Poet Laureate in the City of Glendale, California. His essays have appeared in *The New York Times, Los Angeles Review of Books, Miami Herald, The Baltimore Sun, Lapham's Quarterly, Outside Magazine*, and elsewhere; and his poetry has appeared in *The Los Angeles Press; No, Dear; The Poetry Lighthouse*; *Ararat* magazine; and beyond. Wartanian has taught writing to veterans at the Manhattan VA, incarcerated writers at Rikers Island, youth in Armenia, and undergraduates at Columbia University, where he earned an M.F.A. in writing. He is the recipient of grants and fellowships from the Fulbright Program, Eurasia Partnership Foundation, and Humanity in Action. For Pacific Standard Time ART, Wartanian has collaborated with creative technologists from NASA's Jet Propulsion Laboratory on "Earth Speaks," an interactive poetry installation exhibited during the group showcase *Blended Worlds: Experiments in Interplanetary Imagination* at the Brand Library & Art Center from September 2024 to January 2025.

A multi-instrumentalist, composer, lyricist, and singer-songwriter, Wartanian has performed internationally and released two full-length albums of original music: *Pushkin Street* and *Critical Distance*, an instrumental composition that has been described as "absolutely fresh," "poignant," and "sophisticated," catching the ear of Oscilloscope Laboratories who tapped Wartanian to compose film trailer music for the indie hit *The Tale of King Crab*. In 2023, tracks from *Critical Distance* were used to soundtrack a production of William Saroyan's Pulitzer-winning drama *The Time of Your Life* (dir. Jennifer Chang) staged by the UCLA Theater Department. Wartanian has shared the stage with the likes of Future Islands, Amir ElSaffar, and Kelly Bell Band. He has also performed on stage and in the studio with Grammy Award-winners Mary Youngblood and MB Gordy. He wrote the music and lyrics for vocalist Eileen Khatchadourian, who performed his compositions in London, Berlin, Istanbul, and Beirut.

Wartanian is the proud grandson and great-grandson of Armenian genocide survivors, the son of Armenian parents from Lebanon, and, with his siblings, the first generation in his family to be born in the United States (Baltimore). He founded Letters for Peace in 2017, and currently serves on the advisory board of the International Armenian Literary Alliance.

Index of Photographs and Poems

Fowler Museum at UCLA

Silvia Forni
SHIRLEY & RALPH SHAPIRO DIRECTOR

Guy Wheatley
DEPUTY DIRECTOR

Pejman Aklagi
MUSEUM ATTENDANT

Kate Anderson
MELLON COLLECTIONS & CONSERVATION ASSISTANT

Gassia Armenian
CURATOR AND RESEARCH ASSOCIATE

MANUEL Baltodano
HEAD OF SECURITY

Sam Bartels
TECHNICAL SUPPORT CONSULTANT

Marina Belozerskaya
MANAGING EDITOR

Allison Bowman
EXECUTIVE ASSISTANT

Michal Broomfield
FINANCIAL SERVICES ANALYST

Sarah Chenault
ASSISTANT PROJECT MANAGER

Don Cole
DIRECTOR OF PHOTOGRAPHY

Phil Curtis
GRANTS MANAGER

Christian de Brer
HEAD OF CONSERVATION

Kathy DiGenova
MUSEUM STORE MANAGER

Bridget DuLong
HEAD OF EXHIBITIONS AND PROJECT MANAGEMENT

Luis Figueroa
SECURITY AND OPERATIONS COORDINATOR

Allison Fisher-Olson
REPATRIATION COORDINATOR & CURATOR OF NATIVE AMERICAN CULTURES

Isabel Garcia
HR ANALYST

Erica P. Jones
SENIOR CURATOR OF AFRICAN ARTS

Haley Jones
CURATORIAL ASSISTANT

Irene Kaneshiro
GRAPHIC DESIGNER

Isabella Kelly-Ramirez
COLLECTIONS MANAGER

Amy Landau
DIRECTOR OF EDUCATION AND INTERPRETATION

Gene McHugh
HEAD OF DIGITAL MEDIA

Nathalia Morales-Evanks
DIRECTOR OF COMMUNICATION & MARKETING

Libby O'Kane
ASSISTANT DIRECTOR, EVENTS & MARKETING

Emeth Pittle
MUSEUM VISITOR SERVICES & SECURITY SUPERVISOR (UNTIL MAY 2025)

Patrick A. Polk
SENIOR CURATOR OF LATIN AMERICAN AND CARIBBEAN POPULAR ARTS

Syona Puliady
CURATOR OF TEXTILES OF THE EASTERN HEMISPHERE

Monika Ramnath
ASSISTANT DIRECTOR OF DEVELOPMENT

Rachel Raynor
DIRECTOR OF REGISTRATION AND COLLECTIONS MANAGEMENT

Jeanette Saunders
REGISTRAR

Kimberly Sheets
NAGPRA PROGRAM / ARCHAEOLOGICAL COLLECTIONS MANAGER

Elizabeth Solano
EXHIBITIONS PRODUCTION MANAGER

Benjamin Strauss
DIRECTOR OF DEVELOPMENT

Jessica Strayer
NAGPRA/CALNAGPRA ADMINISTRATIVE MANAGER

Yoo, Hannah
CURATOR OF PUBLIC PROGRAMS

FOLLOWING PAGE:
SOSSI MADZOUNIAN
Mamig (grandma) (detail)